# Vimy

# Vimy

**Vern Thiessen**

**Playwrights Canada Press**
**Toronto • Canada**

PLAYWRIGHTS CANADA PRESS
202-269 Richmond St. W., Toronto, ON M5V 1X1
416.703.0013 • info@playwrightscanada.com • www.playwrightscanada.com

For professional or amateur production rights, please contact:
Michael Petrasek, The Talent House
204A St. George Street, Toronto, ON M5R 2N6
416.960.9686, michael@talenthouse.ca

We acknowledge the financial support of the Canada Council for the Arts, the Ontario
Arts Council (oac), the Ontario Media Development Corporation, and the Government
of Canada through the Canada Book Fund for our publishing activities.

Canada Council Conseil des arts
for the Arts    du Canada

ONTARIO ARTS COUNCIL
CONSEIL DES ARTS DE L'ONTARIO
an Ontario government agency
un organisme du gouvernement de l'Ontario

Canada

Ontario
Ontario Media Development
Corporation

Front cover: Sheldon Elter, photo by David Cooper
Back cover: Daniela Vlaskalic, photo by David Cooper
Production Editor: Michael Petrasek
Cover design: JLArt

Library and Archives Canada Cataloguing in Publication

Thiessen, Vern
    Vimy / Vern Thiessen.

A play.
ISBN 978-0-88754-781-2

    1. Vimy Ridge, Battle of, France, 1917--Drama.  I. Title.

PS8589.H4524V54 2008        C812'.54        C2008-900405-1

First edition: March 2008. Third printing: July 2014.
Printed and bound by Imprimerie Gauvin, Gatineau

# Table of Contents

"We must not accept the memory of states as our own. Nations are not communities and never have been. The history of any country... conceals fierce conflicts of interest."

—Howard Zinn

"One spring day near Vimy Ridge
I very nearly crossed the Bridge
Which leads to Heaven or Hell
For I tried to stop a Fritz shell
But now in Heaven I must be
For around me angels do I see
Protecting me from further harm
For I am bruised and short one arm."

—Sgt. Sid Unwin, May 27, 1917.
Unwin was in the 6th Brigade,
Canadian Field Artillery, Second
Division. He died June 29 of that year.

"If this is your country, where are your stories?
Tell me your stories..."

—attributed to a Blood elder, speaking
to a newly arrived white man, claiming
Canada as "his country."

## Playwright's Note

*Vimy* is not a play about war. It does not ask whether war is right or wrong, nor does it criticize or defend war, past or present. It does not ask whether a battle like the one fought at Vimy Ridge is worth the tremendous commitment and profound sacrifices made by the men and women involved.

Rather, in conceiving *Vimy*, I wanted to crawl inside one small corner of a large offensive and explore something different. I wanted to discover how small actions can define us as individuals and as a nation. This journey gave birth to many questions: Why do we pass over some moments in our history yet mythologize others? Why do we suppress some events while others scorch themselves into our minds? Is there a gap between our memory as a country and our recollection as individuals? What is the no-man's-land between reality and memory, truth and dream, history and mythology? These are the questions that arose as I researched and wrote *Vimy*.

I don't have any more answers than when I started. Like the characters in the play, I can only search for resolutions. And like them, if I keep searching, I may find a little peace.

—Vern Thiessen
New York City, 2007

## Historical Notes

- The battle at Vimy Ridge took place April 9 (Easter Monday) to 12, 1917. It was part of the larger Arras Offensive in the spring of that year. Most of the battle was fought (and won) in the first day.

- It was the first time four divisions of Canadian troops fought together.

- Over 97,000 Canadians were assembled to prepare for the battle of Vimy Ridge, including sappers, infantrymen, signalers, tunnellers, engineers, communication experts, cooks, etc. The total number of Canadians stationed at Vimy Ridge was greater than the population of Vancouver at the time.

- Soldiers came from across Canada, but most volunteers hailed from Western Canada. Some were recent immigrants from Britain, Asia and other countries.

- Over 15,000 men (mostly Canadians) went over the top in the first wave on April 9, 1917.

- There were 10,602 casualties at Vimy Ridge; 3,598 men died.

- These casualties were considered "light" at the time. A year earlier at the Somme, over 20,000 Empire troops died in a single day with a total of more than 500,000 casualties in one month. Later in 1917, at Passchendale, more than 400,000 Empire soldiers would be killed or wounded.

- Four Victoria Crosses were given to Canadian soldiers who fought at Vimy Ridge.

- Twenty-three Canadians were executed by their own men during the Great War for desertion, cowardice or other military crimes. At least four of these men were sentenced to death, in part, for failing to take part in the battle at Vimy Ridge.

- It has been argued aggressively by noted historians and average Canadians alike that Vimy Ridge was the symbolic birth of Canada as a nation. However, in a poll conducted by *The Globe and Mail* in 2002, only 36 per cent of Canadians could name Vimy Ridge as the most significant Canadian victory of the Great War.

- One in three Native men (Aboriginal, First Nations, Métis) volunteered to serve in the Great War. In total, approximately four thousand Native men served overseas. Three hundred died in battle, not including many who died of disease and tuberculosis on their return from the field. Native men received many medals and citations for bravery. Native people also donated more than $44,000 from 1914–1918, a very large sum at the time. Paradoxically, the last residential school was not closed until 1998.

- Approximately 3,100 Canadian women served as nurses in the Canadian Army Nurses Corps during the Great War. Forty-six nursing sisters died as a result of war-action, injury, or disease. The Women's Franchise Act was passed in 1918 permitting all women citizens to vote in federal elections.

## Acknowledgements

*Vimy* was written with the generous assistance of the Citadel Theatre Play Development Program, the Alberta Foundation for the Arts and the Canada Council for the Arts. Thanks also to the Banff playRites Colony 2004 and 2005, the Department of Drama at the University of Alberta and to the Whyte Museum of the Canadian Rockies.

Other crucial support was given by Julian Arnold, Sarah Polkinghorne, Scott Sharplin, Kenneth Williams, Elizabeth Ludwig, Iris Turcott, Ron Jenkins, Ruth Dyckfehderau, Bev Brett, Billy MacLellan and all the actors, directors and dramaturges who have participated in the development of this play. A special thanks to Sharon Richardson, Simon Godly, Brian Dooley, James Macdonald and Bob Baker.

Although *Vimy* is a work of fiction, it is based on factual events and inspired by real Canadians who served in the Great War. They include the following men and women, many of whom fought at Vimy Ridge, or dealt with its aftermath: Archibald John Polson, Sid Unwin, Harold Panabaker, Jean Brillant, Mike Mountain-Horse, Lawrence Gass, Blanchard Gass, Harold Saunders, Clare Gass, Alice MacKinnon, Paul Metevier and William Alexander.

Several books and historical references were highly influential, among them: *My People, The Bloods* by Mike Mountain-Horse; *Vimy* by Pierre Burton; *The Great War and Modern Memory* by Paul Fussel; *The War Diary of Clare Gass* edited by Susan Mann; *Vimy Ridge 1917* by Alexander Turner and Peter Dennis; the writings of Will R. Bird; press quotes from *The New York Times, New York Tribune, The Guardian*; and the Canadian official history of the Great War, available through the Department of National Defence. I am indebted to them all for doing much of my homework for me.

*Vimy* is also influenced by composers such as Vaughan Williams (particularly his *Pastoral* symphony and *The Lark Ascending*) as well as lesser known, but equally influential, folk songs of the time. The Great War poets—Owen, Rosenberg, Sassoon, Brooke and Thomas, as well as many anonymous "trench poets"—were very important to my research.

## Production Notes

Though the play is based on historical incidents, it is not a naturalistic play. Theatricality and non-realism in staging, sound, costume, lighting and design are encouraged. Although the play is poetic at times, it should be played without sentimentality or reverence.

Act One should run sixty-five minutes. Act Two should run approximately forty-five minutes.

### Song/Translations

"Here We Are, Here We Are Again" is by F. Wheeler (1915). To the author's knowledge, it is in the public domain.

French translations are by Brian Dooley with assistance from Vincent Hoss-Desmarais, and are used here with permission.

Both the song's author and the translators should be credited in the house program of any production.

*Vimy* had its world premiere at the Citadel Theatre in Edmonton on October 25, 2007. It played on the Maclab Stage with the following company:

| | |
|---|---|
| **CLARE** | Daniela Vlaskalic |
| **WILL** | Mat Busby |
| **SID** | Phil Fulton |
| **J.P./BERT** | Vincent Hoss-Desmarais |
| **MIKE/CLAUDE** | Sheldon Elter |
| **LAURIE** | Billy MacLellan |

| | |
|---|---|
| Director | James MacDonald |
| Co-Designer | Bretta Gerecke |
| Co-Designer | Narda McCarroll |
| Composer and Sound Design | Dave Clarke |
| Dramaturge | Brian Dooley |
| Dialect Coach | Meredith Scott |
| Stage Manager | Michelle Chan |
| Assistant Stage Manager | Tracey Byrne |
| Apprentice Stage Manager | Lauren Ignacz |

| | |
|---|---|
| Artistic Director | Bob Baker |
| Managing Director | Penny Ritco |
| Director of Production | Dave Horner |
| Technical Director | Bill Heron |
| Company Manager | Peni Christopher |

## Characters

**CLARE**     A nurse with the Canadian Army Nurses Corps. They were commonly reffered to by soldiers as "Bluebirds." She is from Shubenacadie, Nova Scotia. She is in her late 20s or early 30s.

**MIKE**      An infantryman with the 10th Battalion, 2nd Brigade, 1st Division. He is a Blood Indian from Standoff, Alberta. In his 20s. He suffers from the effects of a gas attack.

**JEAN-PAUL** (J.P.) An infantryman with the 22nd Battalion ("The Van Doos"), 5th Brigade, 2nd Division. He is a butcher from Montreal, Quebec. In his 20s. He suffers from shell shock.

**WILL**      An infantryman with the Royal Canadian Regiment, 7th Brigade, 3rd Division. He is a canoe maker from Renfrew, Ontario. In his 20s. He suffers the effects of shrapnel to his arm and upper body.

**SID**       An infantryman with the 44th Battalion, 10th Brigade, 4th Division. He is a construction worker from Winnipeg, Manitoba. In his 20s. He has been blinded and suffers head injuries as well as tuberculosis.

**LAURIE**    A soldier with the Nova Scotia Highlanders, 85th Battalion, 11th Brigade, 4th Division. He is a mining engineer—a graduate of McGill University—but his home is Nova Scotia.

**CLAUDE**    A friend of J.P. He may be doubled with Mike.

**BERT**      Brother to Mike. He may be doubled with J.P.

## ACT ONE

*Four beds—as if a cross.*

*Five men—as if spirits.*

*From away—thunder.*

*CLARE—speaks to LAURIE.*

CLARE  (*smiling*) Dawn. The sun rising red.

Sitting on the cliffs at Five Islands. Surrounded by pines. Looking over Fundy. Watching the sea rush in. Imagining old Glooscap standing on that spot, making the tide turn `round in the bay.

*The thunder—closer.*

It's like a tide, this war. This war's a tide, biting the land, chewing the earth, smacking her lips on the muddy soil, dark and wet.

*The men—become present.*

Boys flood the ground of no-man's-land, streaming toward the Front, like salt water, shoaling up, rising higher and higher until...

*A loud clap—as if a shell bursting.*

*Flares—as if the northern lights.*

*The present—slowly floods her memory.*

The tide turns `round, and a stream of bloodied boys and mangled men surges backward toward me.

*The men—their injuries taking hold.*

Broken bones and blindness. Gas and gangrene. Shrapnel and shredded flesh. Shell shock and shaken.

*The men—sink into their beds.*

*A burst of thunder and guns.*

SID  Get `im off me, get `im—!

J.P.  Dépêche-toi, dépêche-toi, Claude! [*Hurry-up, Hurry-up, Claude!*]

**CLARE**     Laurie…?

*But he is gone.*

† † †

*Day.*

*WILL opens his eyes—groggy.*

*MIKE is awake—wheezing.*

*J.P. stares—in a trance.*

*SID asleep—his eyes bandaged.*

*WILL—sees MIKE.*

**WILL**      Got a smoke?

*Pause.*

**MIKE**      Couple left I think.

*MIKE, wheezing—leans slowly over to the table.*

*He grabs the smokes.*

*With effort, chucks them at WILL's bed.*

*They land.*

**WILL**      Thanks.

**MIKE**      Can't smoke 'em now anyhow.

*WILL tries picking up the smokes.*

*His injured arm reminds him to use the other.*

**WILL**      Got a match?

**MIKE**      …Sorry.

**WILL**      Well ain't we a pair. You can't smoke and I got no match.

*They chuckle quietly—it hurts.*

*WILL looks to J.P.—he wants a match.*

*(to J.P.)* Hey.

*No response.*

Hey.

> *No response.*

Hey buddy.

**MIKE** He ain't talkin'. Tried.

> *WILL ditches the smoke.*

**WILL** Who you with?

**MIKE** 10th Battalion.

**WILL** 1st Division?

**MIKE** Yeah.

**WILL** How you fare?

> *Pause.*

**MIKE** Don' know.

> *Pause.*

**WILL** What happened?

> *Pause.*

**MIKE** Not sure. Can't remember.

> *Pause.*

**WILL** *(of J.P.)* Him?

**MIKE** Van Doos, I think. French.

**WILL** *(of SID)* Him?

**MIKE** Don' know.

**WILL** Looks familiar.

**MIKE** Yeah?

> *WILL stares at SID.*

Who *you* with?

**WILL** Rifles.

**MIKE** 3rd Division?

*WILL nods.*

How you fare?

*Pause.*

**WILL** Don' know.

**MIKE** What happened?

**WILL** Not sure. Can't remember.

*They chuckle—it hurts.*

**MIKE** Where you from then?

**WILL** Renfrew. Near Ottawa. You?

**MIKE** Standoff. Near Lethbridge.

*Pause.*

**WILL** Boy oh boy. What I wouldn't give for a Labatt's now, eh?

**MIKE** Or a Lowney's.

**WILL** Or a bowl a' Saskatoons.

**MIKE** Or a girl!

*CLARE—with food trays.*

**CLARE** Mornin'.

**WILL** Hey.

**MIKE** Mornin'.

**CLARE** Porridge?

**WILL** Porridge?

**MIKE** Hot?

**CLARE** Hot as you can stand it. Saunders.

**WILL** Thanks, Sister.

**CLARE** Goodstriker.

**MIKE** Thanks, Bluebird.

**CLARE** What about you?

*J.P. stares.*

Private Metivier? You want some porridge?

MIKE   He ain't talkin'.

WILL   We already tried.

*She sees SID — checks his I.D.*

CLARE   Polson?

WILL   ...Polson?

CLARE   Sidney?

*No response.*

MIKE   Looks like he ain't talking either.

*They eat — the first real meal in days.*

WILL   Hm...

MIKE   Hm mm....

CLARE   You... you boys at Arras?

WILL   Vimy.

CLARE   Vimy?

MIKE   Me too.

CLARE   Either of you Highlanders?

WILL   Sorry.

MIKE   Not me.

*SID wakes — coughing.*

SID   *(agitated)* ...Get `im off me, get `im...

CLARE   Shh, it's all right...

SID   *(panicked)* Can't see... can't see!

CLARE   Shhhh. It's all right. You're in hospital. We're just letting them heal.

*SID drifts off.*

*WILL stares at him.*

*MIKE notices.*

*CLARE—clears up the breakfast while:*

MIKE       You know him?

WILL       Don' know. Funny, how you forget things.

MIKE       Not me. My memory's like a trap. *(his head)* It's all stuck in here.

*A shell—or a memory—exploding:*

LAURIE     Brave, this one.

WILL       One, two, three, glide…

CLARE      Laurie…?

MIKE       Bert? Wait for me!

LAURIE     It's all stuck in here.

† † †

*Night.*

*A loud crash—thunder.*

J.P.       *(screaming)* AHHH. AHHHH.

*The others stir, but do not wake.*

CLARE      Shhh, shhh.

J.P.       J'peux pas l'faire… j'peux pas… [*I can't do it. I can't…*]

CLARE      Shhh.

*CLARE takes his face in her hands.*

C'est juste le tonnerre. Il n'y a pas de danger. [*It's only thunder. You're safe now.*]

*Pause—as J.P. calms.*

J.P.       Ah… un ange. [*Ah… an angel.*]

CLARE      Non—seulement une fille de Shubenacadie. [*No—just a girl from Shubenacadie.*]

J.P.       Un ange qui parle français! [*An angel who speaks French!*]

| | |
|---|---|
| **CLARE** | Oooh, my French is very rusty. |
| | *J.P.—his hands shaking.* |
| **J.P.** | Mes mains, elles… [*My hands, they…*] |
| **CLARE** | Regarde-moi… [*Look at me…*] |
| **J.P.** | Elles sentent comme, comme… [*They smell like, like…*] |
| **CLARE** | Regarde-moi. [*Look at me.*] |
| **J.P.** | I can't go back, I can't go… |
| **CLARE** | You'll be sent home before you know it. |
| **J.P.** | …Yeah? |
| **CLARE** | A little shell shock. That's all. |
| **J.P.** | …Yeah? |
| **CLARE** | You're gonna be fine. Know why? |
| **J.P.** | Wh–why? |
| **CLARE** | You got me as a nurse. Know why I'm a good nurse? |
| **J.P.** | Wh–why? |
| **CLARE** | J'ai étudié à Montréal. [*I trained in Montreal.*] |
| **J.P.** | *(smiles)* Ah, Montreal! |
| **CLARE** | *(smiles)* Something to eat? Tu veux quelque chose à manger? [*Some food?*] |
| | *J.P.—nods.* |
| | *He takes the spoon, eats.* |
| | *She helps him.* |
| **J.P.** | *(eating)* Mmm. |
| **CLARE** | Better than bully beef, eh? |
| **J.P.** | Mmm. |
| **CLARE** | Looks like you have an appetite! That's good. |
| | *He eats.* |
| | *She is about to leave.* |

*But then:*

CLARE   You, you ever meet any of the Highlanders, Jean-Paul?

J.P.    Highlanders?

CLARE   Yeah.

J.P.    No, miss. Me, Vingt-deux. We...

*He shakes.*

*She steadies his hands.*

Smell my hands.

*She smells.*

They smell like...?

CLARE   Like...?

J.P.    *(smiles)* Liver and steak.

*He smells.*

Smell my hands. They smell like...?

CLARE   Like...?

J.P.    *(smiles)* Sausage and bacon.

Me? My friend Claude...?

*MIKE sits up—coughs.*

We work in my pa's butcher shop. East end.

*MIKE becomes CLAUDE.*

CLAUDE  Jean-Paul!

J.P.    *(to MIKE)* Viens t'en! [*Come on!*]

CLARE   What's that?

J.P.    Dépêche-toi, Claude! [*Hurry up, Claude!*]

CLARE   Jean-Paul?

† † †

**CLAUDE**  Ça ne me tente pas d'aller le voir. [*I don't want to!*] Why do we hafta go?

**J.P.**  Come on, Claude!

*They arrive at a gathering.*

Look at all these people. There's Wilfred Laurier! He's going to make a speech!

**CLAUDE**  Laurier? That boring old fart?!

**J.P.**  What's wrong with you, old friend.

**CLAUDE**  Nothing, *old friend.*

**J.P.**  You wanna wait `til the Huns come sailing down the St. Lawrence?

**CLAUDE**  This is an Anglo war. Everyone knows that. You know what they're doin' in Ontario? French: banned in schools. You wanna fight for that, Jean-Paul?

**J.P.**  No, I wanna fight *against* it. If we don't fight now, we're all gonna be talking *German*, never mind English.

**CLAUDE**  You're crazy.

**J.P.**  No, I just don't wanna be a butcher for the rest of my life.

**CLAUDE**  What's *that* supposed to mean.

**J.P.**  You know what it means. Means my grandpa was a butcher and my pa is a butcher, and now *I'm* a butcher, too. Means I'm sick of being looked at like I'm dirt by every Anglo I meet. Means I'm sick of girls teasing you `cause your English isn't so good. Means I'm sick of my hands smelling like meat all the time. Means I want something better.

**CLAUDE**  Fighting's not going to help.

**J.P.**  Better than doing nothing.

**CLAUDE**  Maybe.

| | |
|---|---|
| **J.P.** | They're starting a new regiment. The 22nd. Le Vingt-Deuxième. At Valcartier. All French Canadians, Claude. All French! |
| **CLAUDE** | *(tempted)* ...I don't know... |
| **J.P.** | Come on. Me and you. Let's show the Anglos who can really fight. |
| **CLAUDE** | What about your pa's shop? |
| **J.P.** | Hey, we'll be done with the Huns so fast, Pa won't even know we were gone! |

*He touches MIKE, who coughs.*

Envoye, qu'est-ce que t'en dis? [*What'dya say?*]

| | |
|---|---|
| **MIKE** | Eh...? |
| **J.P.** | Eh, ami? [*Eh, friend?*] |
| **MIKE** | You talking to me? |
| **J.P.** | J'faisais juste... [*I, I was just...*] |
| **MIKE** | You *starin'* at me, Frenchman?! |
| **CLARE** | It's all right. Go to sleep now. |

*MIKE sinks back into his bed.*

| | |
|---|---|
| **J.P.** | I was... |
| **CLARE** | It's okay. You were... dreaming. |
| **J.P.** | Yeah. Dreaming. |
| **CLARE** | Rest. |

*She starts to leave.*

| | |
|---|---|
| **J.P.** | ...Miss? |
| **CLARE** | ...Yes? |
| **J.P.** | You, you got a boyfriend? |

*LAURIE is there.*

† † †

LAURIE   Will ya take a gander at the stems on that one, wha'?

CLARE   ...I beg your—?

LAURIE   You heard me.

CLARE   Well, I never!

LAURIE   "Well, I never!" Look, just `cause you're Clare Lewis from Shubenacadie, Nova Scotia doesn't mean—

CLARE   How did you—?

LAURIE   Lawrence McLean.

CLARE   Lawrence...

LAURIE   Upper Stewiacke.

CLARE   Upper—

LAURIE   Myself and your brother Blanchard—

CLARE   Laurie! *Laurie* McLean!

LAURIE   Present.

CLARE   Laurie McLean who got into some hot water when he took Blanchard's little sister—

LAURIE   That's you.

CLARE   *(fierce)*Yes, me—ten at the time I might add—took me and pushed me off the walking bridge into the freezing cold creek. *That* Laurie McLean.

LAURIE   We were attempting to ascertain the rate of descent when a falling object—

CLARE   Oh I remember the rate of descent all right, being the one, ya know, *descending*. I remember the bridge and the push and the cold I caught, I remember every detail, it's all burned deep into my memory, it's all stuck in here *(her head)*, Laurie McLean from Upper Stewiacke, Nova Scotia!

LAURIE   Whoa now. Hang on, hang on. I'm sorry about that, Clare. I really am. We was right foolish.

CLARE   I'll say.

| | |
|---|---|
| **LAURIE** | How is good old Blanch? |
| **CLARE** | Taking care of Mother. While I'm at McGill. |
| **LAURIE** | *(her uniform, impressed)* Nursing, she is! *(incredulous)* Not goin' overseas? |
| **CLARE** | When I'm done. |
| **LAURIE** | Brave, this one. |
| **CLARE** | They need people. |
| **LAURIE** | Need people in engineering, too. Doesn't mean I'm signing up. |
| **CLARE** | *(impressed, but not showing)* Engineering? |
| **LAURIE** | Surveying next week. |
| **CLARE** | Back home? |
| **LAURIE** | Rockies. Dominion Land Survey. |
| **CLARE** | Oooh. "Dominion Land Survey." |
| **LAURIE** | Speaking of... how's your French. |
| **CLARE** | Passable. Why? |
| **LAURIE** | There's an outfitter see, down in Place Jacques-Cartier, and... |
| **CLARE** | Yes? |
| **LAURIE** | I was hoping to find someone, ya know, to help, with the buying of supplies, before I go. |
| **CLARE** | Why me? |
| **LAURIE** | `Cause I... I... |
| **CLARE** | Tu ne parles pas français? [*You don't speak French?*] |
| **LAURIE** | What's that? |

> *CLARE—a small smile.*
>
> *J.P.—becomes present.*

| | |
|---|---|
| | And afterwards...? |
| **J.P.** | Miss? |

**CLARE**   Yes?

**LAURIE**   Maybe I could…

**J.P.**   Miss?

**CLARE**   …yes?

**LAURIE**   *(smiles)* Get you drunk. As a thank you.

**J.P.**   I take you back to Montreal, you and me?

**LAURIE/J.P.**   What'd'ya say…?

*LAURIE is gone.*

**CLARE**   Men. Foolish.

† † †

*Time passes.*

*Then:*

† † †

**J.P.**   Any mail, miss?

**CLARE**   Sorry.

**MIKE**   Nothing?

**CLARE**   That's what I said.

*She sits beside WILL, examines him.*

**J.P.**   *(cursing)* Mausus…

**MIKE**   Expecting something?

**J.P.**   Maybe. Maybe a discharge, or—?

**MIKE**   Discharge?!

**J.P.**   And what's wrong with that?

**MIKE**   Ha, ha…

**J.P.**   What are you laughing at?

**SID**   J.P.

**MIKE**   Discharge? Ha ha ha!

| | |
|---|---|
| **J.P.** | I said, what are you laughing at?! |
| **SID** | J.P. |
| **J.P.** | ...Yeah? |
| **SID** | Help me with a letter would ya? |
| **J.P.** | *(his hands, shaking)* My writing, it's not so good, you know? |
| **SID** | Just do a Whizbang for me. Please? |

*J.P. goes—glaring at MIKE.*

| | |
|---|---|
| **CLARE** | How's the arm? |
| **WILL** | Aches. |
| **CLARE** | Hurts? |
| **WILL** | No. Aches. |
| **CLARE** | Let's see. |
| **WILL** | *(pain)* Ah. |
| **CLARE** | What about your chest? |
| **WILL** | Hurts. |
| **CLARE** | Aches? |
| **WILL** | No. HURTS. |
| **CLARE** | Nasty stuff, shrapnel. |
| **WILL** | Hoped for a blighty, didn't think it'd— |
| **CLARE** | Two more inches and it would've taken out a piece of your heart. |
| **WILL** | Wish it would've. |
| **CLARE** | Now now. You're a lucky man, Will. |
| **SID** | ...Will? |

*WILL is silent.*

Will?

*WILL is silent.*

That you?

**WILL** *(forced)* Yeah, that's my name.

**SID** It's Sid.

>*WILL is silent.*

From Winnipeg. Don't you remember?

**WILL** Got me confused with another guy.

**SID** Ya sure?

**WILL** Sorry, bud.

**SID** *(confused)* It's just that your voice—

**CLARE** Sid. I'll get you fresh bandages.

>*J.P. comes back with the field card.*

>*CLARE leaves, staring at WILL.*

**J.P.** Okay: Whizbang! Sid...

**SID** Polson.

**J.P.** Polson. Who you with?

**SID** 44th Battalion.

**J.P.** Winnipeg?

**SID** Yeah.

**J.P.** 4th Division?

**SID** Yeah.

**J.P.** How'd you fare?

**SID** Don't know.

**J.P.** What happened?

**SID** Not sure. Can't remember.

>*MIKE laughs.*

**J.P.** What's so funny?

>*MIKE laughs harder.*

I said, what's so funny.

*MIKE laughs.*

What's so funny, Indian!

*A tense pause.*

**MIKE**  Gotta piss.

*MIKE makes his way off—slow.*

**J.P.**  Which one you wanna keep: "I am quite well." "I have been admitted into hospital."

**SID**  Admitted to hospital.

**J.P.**  Check. "Sick" or "Wounded."

**SID**  Wounded.

**J.P.**  Check. "Am going on well" or "Hope to be discharged soon."

**SID**  Going on well.

**J.P.**  Check. "I have received no letter from you…" "lately" or "for a long time."

**SID**  For a… for a long time.

**J.P.**  …anything else?

**SID**  Keep "Letter follows at first opportunity."

**J.P.**  Sign on the line, my friend.

*J.P., his hands shaky, helps SID sign.*

Whiz! Bang! Winnipeg here we come.

**SID**  No. It's okay. I'll send it later.

*SID coughs.*

**J.P.**  Water?

*SID nods.*

*J.P. leaves.*

*WILL and SID are alone.*

† † †

*SID becomes active, animated, charming.*

**SID**  Hot today.

> *WILL looks out.*

Hot.

> *WILL looks out.*

Mind if I...?

> *WILL says nothing.*

Beautiful here.

Whiteshell.

Nicest part of Manitoba, I tell ya.

> *Flies.*

`Cept the stupid flies. Worse than Ontario. What is it about Ontario. Soon as you hit Kenora, the flies get twice as big, twice as bad, and three times as mean. Somethin' `bout Ontario makes the flies mean. Where ya from then?

**WILL**  Ontario.

**SID**  Oh.

Me? Winnipeg.

> *WILL listens but says nothing.*

You working the train or the water?

**WILL**  Water.

**SID**  Me too. Buildin' tunnels for the water. Fresh clean water. Ninety-two miles from the bottom of Shoal Lake to the top of the Eaton's building.

> *WILL listens but says nothing.*

They say it'll take a thousand men four years.

> *WILL listens but says nothing.*

But now with the war…. Who knows, eh?

*WILL listens but says nothing.*

You don't say much, do ya?

**WILL**   I like being alone.

**SID**   Oh.

*But he doesn't move.*

*WILL regards him.*

*Finally, he relents:*

**WILL**   All I got to say is… I hope the fine people of Winnipeg are happy with their water.

*He smiles. So does SID.*

**SID**   Sid.

**WILL**   Will.

*They shake hands.*

**SID**   So. You signin' up?

**WILL**   Maybe.

**SID**   Me, I figure I can help my country by makin' sure they got water to drink.

**WILL**   Right.

**SID**   Though some days, when we're tunneling, and I'm throwin' down the pick twelve hours, I think, to hell with all this water, to hell with Winnipeg, to hell with it. Rather be in a trench somewhere in France. Ya know?

**WILL**   My old man…

**SID**   Yeah?

**WILL**   Fought in the Boer War…

**SID**   Yeah?

**WILL**   Says it's my duty. He fought to keep the country free. Now it's my turn.

| | |
|---|---|
| **SID** | Believe that? |
| **WILL** | I don't know. Maybe. It's different times now, eh? |
| **SID** | For sure. |
| **WILL** | I want something different, but he doesn't get that. |
| **SID** | My folks, they don' get me neither. |
| **WILL** | No? |
| **SID** | No. |
| **WILL** | Why's that. |
| **SID** | I don' know.... I... |

> *SID takes out a postcard.*

| | |
|---|---|
| | See this. That's where I wanna go. |
| **WILL** | Where? |
| **SID** | Bora Bora. |
| **WILL** | Bora...? |
| **SID** | Bora Bora. Know where that is? |
| **WILL** | *(no)* Uh uh. |
| **SID** | Tahiti. An island. |
| **WILL** | Why you wanna go there? |
| **SID** | Why?! Look at that! Coconut trees. Sandy beaches. Warm blue water. You know what the average temperature is on Bora Bora? |
| **WILL** | Uh... |
| **SID** | Eighty degrees! Eighty degrees all year round. Know what the average temperature in Winnipeg is? |
| **WILL** | Colder? |
| **SID** | You know it! |
| | I'm gonna make enough money digging these tunnels, and then bang! On a steamer to Bora Bora. Eat fish straight from the ocean. Drink rum and coconut |

milk. Find me... someone special. And just... lie there.

WILL    Me, I wanna live in a canoe.

SID     Canoeing eh?

WILL    Build my own.

SID     Really?

WILL    Source Lake.
Algonquin way.
Nothin' but water and white pines.

SID     Yeah?

WILL    *(searching for the words)* It's like...
It's like you're gliding, ya know?
Like you're, you're a bird or something.

And everywhere you look, you see the story of the place:
The trees.
The rocks.
The water...

At Barron Canyon, the river gets restless.
Wants to keep moving.

So you keep gliding:
Along the Algonquin Highlands.
Across the South Madawaska.
Down the Ottawa River.
'Til you perch yourself—on a branch near Arnprior.

And you're home.

So. Day off? I'm goin' paddling.

        *SID is awestruck.*

You?

SID     Huh?

WILL    What you gonna do, day off?

SID     I don't know.
Head back to Winnipeg, I guess.

Ya know:
Sit around.
Pass the time.
With my folks.

*He stares at his postcard.*

Well… better get back to work.

| | |
|---|---|
| **WILL** | Wanna come? |
| **SID** | Huh? |
| **WILL** | Canoeing. |
| **SID** | …Really? |
| **WILL** | Course. |
| **SID** | You sure? `Cause I… |
| **WILL** | Come. |
| **SID** | I don't know, I… |
| **WILL** | What? |

*Pause.*

| | |
|---|---|
| **SID** | I thought you liked being alone. |
| **WILL** | Thought I didn't say much either. |

*They smile.*

† † †

*CLARE enters. She goes to SID.*

| | |
|---|---|
| **CLARE** | All right then. |

*She wraps his eyes.*

| | |
|---|---|
| **SID** | Nurse. |
| **CLARE** | Just a minute. |
| **SID** | Can you deliver this Whizbang for me. |
| **CLARE** | When I'm finished here. |
| **SID** | Nurse? |

CLARE     Just a moment.

SID       It's goin' to Private William Saunders.

          *CLARE stops.*

CLARE     *(careful)* Of course.

          *She takes the Whizbang.*

SID       Thanks.

          *SID coughs, turns over.*

          *CLARE hands the card to WILL.*

          *She starts dressing his wounds.*

WILL      What's gonna happen. With my arm.

CLARE     I don't know.

WILL      `Cause if I can't...

CLARE     I don't know. Honest.

          *Finishes the dressing.*

          There.

WILL      Listen...

          *LAURIE is there.*

          I got this... mess. Stuck inside me. And I feel like it
          ain't ever gonna leave.

LAURIE    Well?

WILL      And I just need time to...

LAURIE    You wanted a story, didn't ya?

WILL      I just need time to...

LAURIE    And it ain't ever gonna leave, Clare...

WILL      Ya know?

          *LAURIE leaves. CLARE nods.*

CLARE     Want a cigarette?

WILL      ...No.

| | |
|---|---|
| **CLARE** | Tot of rum? |
| **WILL** | …No. |
| **CLARE** | Want me… to stay? |
| **WILL** | Na. |
| | I like being alone. |

† † †

*Nightmares.*

| | |
|---|---|
| **SID** | Can't see, can't see… |
| **J.P.** | Mes mains, elles sentent comme… |

† † †

*MIKE is awake—coughing, wheezing.*
*CLARE enters.*

| | |
|---|---|
| **CLARE** | Me'talwle'in? [*You okay?*] |
| **MIKE** | What's that? |
| **CLARE** | Minu'wi'tm, me'talwle'in? [*I said, you okay?*] |
| **MIKE** | What are you…? |
| **CLARE** | Mi'kmaq? From Nova Scotia? |
| **MIKE** | Blood. From Alberta. |
| **CLARE** | Oh! I thought… |
| **MIKE** | What. |
| **CLARE** | It's just that— |
| **MIKE** | We all look alike? |
| **CLARE** | No, that's not what I— |
| **MIKE** | Hey. <br> Bluebird. <br> Pulling your leg. |

*MIKE—laughs, coughs.*

Lungs feel like…

| | |
|---|---|
| **CLARE** | Here. |

> *Some water.*
>
> *He drinks.*

Turn around please.

> *He does. She takes out a stethoscope.*

| | |
|---|---|
| **MIKE** | Dyin' for a smoke. |
| **CLARE** | I don't think that would be wise. |
| **MIKE** | Wisdom and smokin' don' have anything to do with each other. |

> *She listens to his chest.*

How's it you...? Mi'kmaq.

| | |
|---|---|
| **CLARE** | Nova Scotia. Reserve across the road. Take a breath. |
| **MIKE** | *(pain)* Ah! |
| **CLARE** | Whoever invented poison gas should be... |
| **MIKE** | ...Gassed? |
| **CLARE** | Hm. |
| **MIKE** | How's it sound? |
| **CLARE** | Well... |
| **MIKE** | Am I gonna die? |
| **CLARE** | Hope not. |
| **MIKE** | Not gonna send me home, are ya? |
| **CLARE** | What, you wanna go back into the line? |
| **MIKE** | Maybe. |

> *She regards his sanity.*

How long I gotta stay.

| | |
|---|---|
| **CLARE** | 'Til you're better. |
| **MIKE** | Few days? |
| **CLARE** | I think longer. |

| | |
|---|---|
| **MIKE** | Ah, I'm all right, Bluebird. See? |
| | *He tries to go for a jog around the room.* |
| **CLARE** | Whoa now— |
| **MIKE** | Coupla days I'll be— |
| **CLARE** | Lie down, lie— |
| **MIKE** | —good as new, see? |
| | *A coughing fit.* |
| **CLARE** | *(smiles)* Coupla days, huh? |
| | *CLARE helps him lie down.* |
| | *LAURIE appears.* |
| **MIKE** | Don't you sleep? |
| **CLARE** | Better to keep busy. Keeps your mind offa… |
| **LAURIE** | Clare! |
| **MIKE** | Offa what? *(pain)* Ah! |
| **CLARE** | You should be the one sleeping. |
| **MIKE** | Oh I'll sleep all right. And I'll be having mighty fine visions of you! |
| **CLARE** | Men! |
| **MIKE** | Never had a vision, Bluebird? |
| **CLARE** | Ha! |
| **MIKE** | Where I come from, visions are sacred. |
| **CLARE** | Are they now. |
| **MIKE** | Me and my brother. |
| | *J.P. sits up. He is BERT.* |
| **BERT** | Mike! |
| **MIKE** | We had a vision once. |
| **BERT** | Mike! |
| **CLARE** | That right? |

| | |
|---|---|
| **BERT** | Poksa powt, neehsa! [*Come on, brother!*] |
| **MIKE** | You ever been on a mountain, Bluebird? At night. |
| **LAURIE** | Clare! |
| **CLARE** | Uh huh. |
| **MIKE** | Then ya know what I'm talking about. |
| **CLARE** | Sleep. |
| **LAURIE** | Clare, wait up. |

† † †

| | |
|---|---|
| **BERT** | Nitakit, Mike! [*Get up here, Mike!*] |

*MIKE is now healthy and hale.*

| | |
|---|---|
| **MIKE** | Nitakittapoh, Bert! [*I'm comin', Bert!*] |
| **BERT** | We'll camp here tonight. See if we don't see a vision. |
| **MIKE** | Can't we go home? |
| **BERT** | Do what I tell ya! |
| **MIKE** | But we been up and down this mountain four days and three nights, and we haven't seen a vision yet. |
| **BERT** | If you're hunting, don' you look at the trail? |
| **MIKE** | ...yeah |
| **BERT** | ...and don' you smell the air? |
| **MIKE** | ...yeah... |
| **BERT** | And don' you listen for things, that tell you there's an animal close? |
| **MIKE** | ...sure. |
| **BERT** | Same thing here. Nah-kay-iss-tsi-sin naan. [*Ya gotta listen.*] Ya gotta be quiet. If you keeping yakking all the time, you'll never hear or see what we're supposed to hear and see. |
| **MIKE** | But... |
| **BERT** | Don't ya wanna be brave? |

MIKE     But we're runnin' low on food, we're runnin' low on water, and it's cold—

BERT     Being a warrior, being brave, being a man, it don't come easy, Mike. It's gonna cost you something.

*They lie down—stare at the sky.*

Mike…. Look!

MIKE     Northern lights. Have ya ever seen `em like that brother, reds and whites and greens dancing.

BERT     That ain't northern lights.

MIKE     No?

BERT     Look at `em. That's a fire, see?

MIKE     A fire!

BERT     Flames licking the top of Chief Mountain. It's like they're saying:

MIKE     "Go to the fire, boys."

BERT     "Go fight under a sky of fire."

MIKE     "Be warriors."

BERT     Then that's what we're gonna do. We're gonna be brave. You and me. Right?

MIKE     You and me.

LAURIE     Clare, wait up!

BERT     Now that, little brother, is what I call a vision.

† † †

LAURIE     Clare!

CLARE     Just `cause I'm more fit than you.

LAURIE     Are not.

CLARE     Look at you, huffin' and puffin'—couldn't climb a snowbank! How'd you manage to survey the Rockies?

LAURIE     Horses.

CLARE       Ah, horses!

LAURIE      And we weren't after chasing women up a mountain
            neither. Not at night at least.

            *She hits him.*

CLARE       And what about the Hun. You gonna chase them as
            badly as you chase me.

LAURIE      Oh, now I've been told!

CLARE       Yes, now you've been told!

            *He runs after her, catches her, lays her down.*

            Well now, Mr. Surveyor.

LAURIE      Lieutenant Surveyor, please.

CLARE       Lieutenant Surveyor. Can you please tell me about
            this here place we are currently lying on.

LAURIE      Well, this here is Mont Royal, first named in 1535
            by—

CLARE       Nope, nope, nope.

LAURIE      I thought you—?

CLARE       I want to hear the *story* of this place, not how tall it is.

LAURIE      The story of it.

CLARE       What's in its heart. What does it remember.

LAURIE      Remember?

CLARE       Doesn't it remember a man...?

LAURIE      A man...?

CLARE       A man making his way up its side. Comin' to build a
            big cross.

LAURIE      ...Ah...

CLARE       And doesn't it remember how, when it was young,
            its eyes were deep with limestone. And its hair soft
            with pine boughs. And its hips delicate as shale. And
            doesn't it remember the people wandering up from

the city, and smelling the picnics, and watching folks make love in its groves by moonlight...

*He kisses her.*

*She enjoys it.*

*But then: she pulls away.*

LAURIE     What's wrong?

CLARE      You should stay. You shouldn't be—

LAURIE     What, and let you have all the fun? Let you go to war on your own while I stay behind, squattin' on some rock?

CLARE      You know what I mean.

LAURIE     Look, Clare: I want to be close to you. I'd rather be close and in harm's way, than an ocean apart and safe.

CLARE      But what if...

LAURIE     Clare. I'm an engineer. I'll be engineering.

CLARE      Doesn't mean you won't have to fight.

LAURIE     Clare:
Listen to me.
If things get bad...
Well...
I'll just remember.

CLARE      Remember? What'll you remember.

*He appears very serious.*

LAURIE     Your beady eyes

CLARE      Beady!

LAURIE     —and your coarse hair

CLARE      Oh!

LAURIE     —and your big hips!

CLARE      You!

LAURIE   And your temper, and your pride, and your smile as wide as the sea. And that's all I need to see me through, Clare. It's in my memory now.

*A shell bursts in her mind.*

J.P.   *(with below)* J'peux pas l'faire... j'peux pas...

MIKE   *(with below)* Under a sky of fire...

SID   *(with below)* Cold, so cold...

WILL   One, two, three, glide...

*And then it's gone.*

LAURIE   It's all stuck in here. *(his heart)*

†††

*Time passes.*

*Then:*

†††

*The boys—occupy themselves.*

*From away—the ever-present sounds of war.*

*CLARE enters, perhaps with linens.*

J.P.   Any mail, miss?

CLARE   Nothin' but last month's newspaper.

*MIKE elects to take it.*

*CLARE—changes sheets.*

J.P.   Sacre, when are we gonna get some mail!

CLARE   When it comes.

WILL   When can we go outside for a walk.

CLARE   When I tell you.

SID   I could really use a hot bath—

CLARE   Gentlemen! Please!

*From afar—shells.*

| | |
|---|---|
| **MIKE** | *(reading, then)* Can't be! |
| **WILL** | …What. |
| **MIKE** | *(reading)* You won't believe it. |
| **J.P.** | What are you mumbling about! |
| **MIKE** | *(reading)* "The Stanley Cup was awarded last month to… the Seattle Metropolitans?! |

> *Outrage.*

| | |
|---|---|
| **SID** | What?! |
| **J.P.** | Get outta—!! |
| **WILL** | Seattle!? |
| **MIKE** | *(reading snippets)* "The first American team to win the Cup… faced the Montreal Canadiens, outscoring them 19 to 3." |
| **J.P.** | *(cursing)* Batinse de cercueil! |
| **MIKE** | "Frank Foyston, formerly of the Toronto Blueshirts, also scored heavily for Seattle." |
| **J.P.** | Foyston! *(spits)* Traitor. |
| **WILL** | An *American* team? |
| **MIKE** | Cyclone Taylor—now there's a player. |
| **J.P.** | Cyclone—? Anglo hack! |
| **MIKE** | Name me a better player, Frenchman! |
| **J.P.** | Newsey Lalonde! |
| **MIKE** | Newsey Lalonde! |
| **J.P.** | Best player ever lived. |
| **MIKE** | Nobody skates like Taylor! |
| **J.P.** | Nobody scores like Newsey! |
| **WILL** | Seattle? And we're fighting for this country *why*? |
| **MIKE** | Cyclone! |
| **J.P.** | Newsey! |

| | |
|---|---|
| **SID** | The Winnipeg Victorias won the Stanley Cup in— |
| **J.P.** | Winnipeg!? |
| **MIKE** | Beat Montreal! |
| **J.P.** | You don't know what you're talking about. |

*From afar—a shell.*

| | |
|---|---|
| **CLARE** | Hockey was invented in Nova Scotia. |
| **J.P.** | First game with rules, Quebec! |
| **WILL** | Kingston, it was King—! |
| **SID** | The Irish brought it over—! |
| **MIKE** | It was INDIANS first played it. |
| **J.P.** | Is that so? |
| **MIKE** | Lacrosse on ice. |
| **J.P.** | You Indians gotta do everything first, huh? |
| **MIKE** | Been in the country a helluva lot longer than the French. |
| **J.P.** | Not our fault you gave it away. |
| **MIKE** | Gave it—?! |

*A shell—closer.*

| | |
|---|---|
| **CLARE** | Boys... |
| **J.P.** | Why you fighting anyway. |
| **MIKE** | Why?! |
| **J.P.** | What do you care? |
| **MIKE** | Helluva lotta Indians signed up for this war. We got whole reservations don't have a man over eighteen on 'em. Now you tell me, Frenchie, how many of your guys signed up? |
| **J.P.** | My friend Claude and me, that's who! |
| **WILL** | Hey, hey— |
| **SID** | Come on guys— |

| | |
|---|---|
| **MIKE** | *(to J.P.)* All you care about is getting your walking papers. |
| **J.P.** | So what if I do? |
| **MIKE** | Guys are dying out there— |
| **J.P.** | And I'm gonna go home and tell them what a crazy, stupid war this really is. |
| **SID** | All right, all right— |
| **WILL** | That's enough— |
| **MIKE** | You think a little shell shock's gonna get you home, Frenchie? |
| **J.P.** | Shut up ya red-skinned— |
| **MIKE** | 'Cause you'll be the FIRST to get sent back to the line, ya COWARD! |
| **SID** | Whoa! |
| **WILL** | Come on now! |
| **J.P.** | Ferme ta gueule, stupide, salot, enfant de chienne de bâtard...! [*Shut your mouth, you dirty, stupid, son-of-a...!*] |

> *J.P. and MIKE go after each other.*
>
> *Yelling.*
>
> *Finally:*

| | |
|---|---|
| **CLARE** | Stop it! |
| | Stop It! |
| | STOP IT!!! |

> *They separate.*

What is WRONG with you!?

You think I came here for this?

You think I left my, my *life*... for THIS?

> *They are silent.*

*(firm)* You think you're the only ones want to go home? You think you're the only ones want to do good? You think you're the only ones hurtin'? You think you're the only ones who gave up something?

Well you're not. I see dozens of ya every single day. Every DAY. And for every one of you, there's another hundred out there.

So you tell me: why should I bother. Why should I bother putting you back together, if all you're going to do is tear each other apart. You tell me.

*(a real question)* TELL ME?

> *Another shell, lingering, like a memory.*
>
> *They are silent.*
>
> *She moves away.*

✝ ✝ ✝

> *They speak with caution, almost to themselves.*
>
> *CLARE hears them from a distance.*

**WILL**      A whale's back.

> *Pause.*

**MIKE**      A horse's spine.

> *Pause.*

**J.P.**      A muddy bank.

> *Pause.*

**SID**      It starts on the southeast.

**MIKE**      Farbus Woods.

**WILL**      It rises slow.

**MIKE**      A foothill.

**J.P.**      Thelus—shelled to shit.

**SID**      It slopes up, to the peak.

**WILL**      Hill 145.

| | |
|---|---|
| **SID** | It ends on the northwest. |
| **J.P.** | At the Pimple. |

*They begin to listen to each other.*

| | |
|---|---|
| **SID** | The Ridge. |
| **WILL** | Four hundred feet high. |
| **SID** | Seven miles across. |
| **J.P.** | Like an island. |
| **WILL** | Its shoulder leaning in like... |
| **MIKE** | A bank on the Milk River. |
| **SID** | But on top, it's flat... |
| **MIKE** | Like the prairie. |
| **WILL** | Its eastern ridge drops down... |
| **SID** | A tangle of trees filled with... |
| **J.P.** | Huns and... |
| **SID** | Machine guns and... |
| **MIKE** | Wire. |

*They turn to CLARE.*

| | |
|---|---|
| **SID** | Only place in France. |
| **J.P.** | Only *real* place you can see the war. |
| **WILL** | The whole of it. |
| **J.P.** | Is from the top... |
| **SID** | Of Vimy. |
| **MIKE** | Vimy. |
| **WILL** | Vimy. |

† † †

*Time moves like a tide.*

*As CLARE speaks:*

*The boys slowly become whole again.*

*Their injuries vanish.*

*They begin to put on their boots.*

*Perhaps LAURIE lingers in the shadows.*

**CLARE**   It's like a tide, this war: biting the land, chewing the earth, smacking her lips on the muddy soil, dark and wet.

Boys flooding the ground of no-man's-land.
Streaming toward the Front.
Shoaling up.
Higher.
And higher.
And higher...

† † †

*Snare. Or an Aboriginal drum.*

**J.P.**   Finally!

**SID**   Go Winnipeg!

*The boys put on their puttees and belts.*

*CLARE listens to them.*

1914 was...

**WILL**   Ypres.

**MIKE**   My brother was there.

**SID**   1915 was...

**WILL**   Ypres again.

**MIKE**   My brother was there, too.

**SID**   1916?

**WILL**   The Somme.

**MIKE**   ...The Somme.

**J.P.**   La Somme, wow!

**SID**   You been?

| | |
|---|---|
| **MIKE** | What? |
| **SID** | Over the top. |
| **MIKE** | Nope. |
| **SID** | You? |
| **WILL** | *(no)* Uh uh. |
| **MIKE** | You? |
| **SID** | Nope. You? |
| **J.P.** | Finally! |
| **MIKE** | They say there'll be a big offensive. |
| **SID** | Twenty thousand men. |
| **MIKE** | Four divisions. |
| **WILL** | All Canadians, eh. |
| **J.P.** | Take Vimy Ridge. |
| **MIKE** | Brits couldn't take it. |
| **J.P.** | Take Vimy Ridge. |
| **SID** | French couldn't take it. |
| **J.P.** | Emparez-vous de la crête de Vimy! [*Take Vimy Ridge!*] |
| **WILL** | And we're suppose to do it in eight hours. |
| **SID** | Eight hours?! |
| **MEN** | HA, HA, HA! |
| **WILL** | Are they—? |
| **SID** | How in the hell—? |
| **WILL** | This is crazy. |
| **J.P.** | This is what we've been waiting for! |
| **MIKE** | Look at the fightin' Frenchman! |
| **J.P.** | Look, I told you—! |
| **WILL** | All right! `Nough of this bullshit. You boys wanna die? |

| | |
|---|---|
| **J.P.** | No. |
| **MIKE** | No. |
| **WILL** | We're gonna do this our way. Am I right? |
| **SID** | Right. |
| **MIKE** | Right. |
| **WILL** | You? |
| **J.P.** | Hey! Je suis Canadien français. Tu t'en rappelles? [*Hey I'm a French Canadian. Remember?*] |

*Snare.*

*Maps.*

| | |
|---|---|
| **MIKE** | What's this? |
| **SID** | Every guy gets a map. |
| **WILL** | A map? |
| **SID** | A battle plan. |
| **MIKE** | That's different. |
| **SID** | Every guy knows what everybody else is supposed to do, that way, someone goes down— |
| **MIKE** | The next guy can take over. |
| **SID** | Exactly. |
| **J.P.** | How long we got? |
| **SID** | Three months. |

*Snare.*

*They line up for their orders.*

*Focus on MIKE:*

| | |
|---|---|
| **SID** | 1st Division. South slope, easy rise. You got two hours to get to Black Line, another two hours to get to Red Line, another two hours to get to Blue Line, and another hour to get to Brown Line. Seven hours in total to Farbus Wood. That clear? |

ALL      Clear, sir!

> *Snare.*
>
> *Focus on J.P.*

MIKE      2nd Division. Trois heures pour vous rendre à la Ligne Noire, une autre heure pour la Ligne Rouge, deux autres heures jusqu'à la Ligne Bleue—c'est la ville de Thelus. Vous avez six heures pour vous rendre à Thelus. Comprenez? [*Three hours to Black Line, another hour to Red Line, another two to Blue Line—that's the town of Thelus. You got six hours to get to Thelus. Got it?*]

ALL      Oui, Sergent!

> *Snare.*
>
> *Focus on WILL.*

J.P.      3rd Division. Black Line, Red Line—to the top, boys, Hill 145. You got two hours to do it. And you're gonna do it, right?

ALL      Right, sir!

> *Snare.*
>
> *Focus on SID.*

WILL      4th Division. North face. The Black Line and the Pimple. That's all you gotta do. But it's straight up, that's the tough part. Can you do it?

ALL      Yes, sir!

> *Snare.*
>
> *They dig.*
>
> *Focus on SID.*

MIKE      (*to CLARE*) Three months to Zero Day.

J.P.      Keep digging!

SID      What are we diggin' anyway?

WILL      Subways.

| | |
|---|---|
| **MIKE** | Tunnels. |
| **WILL** | Twelve of `em. |
| **SID** | You mean we gotta build twelve subways—? |
| **WILL** | In three months. |
| **MIKE** | At night! |
| **SID** | Came here to get away from a pick and shovel. |
| **J.P.** | Keep digging. `Cause when we're done with these tunnels, and we pop outta those holes like gophers, the Huns, they gonna be very, very surprised, and you're gonna be thankful I busted your butt. |
| **SID** | Coulda stayed at home, finished digging the waterway. |
| **J.P.** | Why is it Winnipeggers are such whiners? |
| **SID** | `Cause it's too cold in the winter and too hot in the summer. `Cause the wind's too hard and the rain's too light. `Cause the skeeters and the snow suck the blood out of you worse than a leech, depending on the season. `Cause it's never just, ya know, WARM. |
| **J.P.** | Winnipeg sounds worse than the war. |

*Snare.*

| | |
|---|---|
| **MIKE** | *(to CLARE)* Two months to Zero Day. |
| **WILL** | Behind the lines... |
| **SID** | We practice: |
| **MIKE** | Like the summer hunt. |
| **J.P.** | Like the Bande de la Cité. |
| **SID** | Like the Winnipeg Victorias playing for the Stanley Cup. |
| **J.P.** | Ha! |
| **WILL** | Not a chance! |
| **SID** | *(whistles their attention)* Practice the Creeping Barrage! |

| | |
|---|---|
| **WILL** | *(oh no)* Not the Creeping Barrage! |
| | *Snare.* |
| | *They practice the Vimy Glide.* |
| | *Focus on WILL:* |
| **SID** | One, two, three, glide... NO! TOO FAST! |
| **WILL** | I'm trying, Cap'n. |
| **SID** | You wanna get killed by your own barrage, Private? |
| **WILL** | No, sir! |
| **SID** | You want that rainstorm of fire, that curtain of hot steel, falling on your head? |
| **WILL** | No, sir! |
| **SID** | No, you want it raining on the Hun's head. You want Fritz pinned to his trench by that barrage while you make your way across no man's land with your bayonet UP! Do you understand! |
| **WILL** | Yes, sir! |
| **SID** | Then don't get ahead of yourself. *Exactly* one hundred yards every three minutes. |
| **WILL** | Yes, Cap'n! |
| **SID** | One, two, three, glide. No, No, NO! |
| **WILL** | Sir!? |
| **SID** | Too slow, too slow! You get behind, you'll lose the men ahead of you!? You want that? |
| **WILL** | No, sir! |
| **SID** | You ever paddle a canoe back home? |
| **WILL** | Who hasn't, sir. |
| **SID** | Know how you navigate a river? |
| **WILL** | Yes, sir. |
| **SID** | Well, then you know what I'm talking about. It's a glide. |

| | |
|---|---|
| **WILL** | One, two— |
| **SID** | Gettin' there. |

    *Snare.*

    *The digging.*

    When's a guy get his bully beef 'round here?

| | |
|---|---|
| **J.P.** | Keep digging! |

    *Snare.*

| | |
|---|---|
| **MIKE** | *(to CLARE)* One month to Zero Day. |

    *Focus on J.P.*

| | |
|---|---|
| **WILL** | You! Private. |
| **J.P.** | Yes, sir. |
| **WILL** | You speak French? |
| **J.P.** | Maybe. Sir. |
| **WILL** | Need help with communications. Those French guys in the Black Watch, the Royals, the Victorias, the Grenadiers, they need to know exactly what's goin' on. |
| **J.P.** | Yes, sir. |

    *The Captain speaks to the men, and J.P. translates into French overtop.*

| | |
|---|---|
| **WILL** | *(with J.P. below)* We got one hundred thousand men here. And we're gonna need each and every one of you. We got: |

Fifty thousand horses to feed.
Twenty-five miles of road to build.
Twenty miles of track to lay.
Twenty-one miles of cable to bury.
Forty-five miles of pipeline to move two million litres of water.
We need to work fast.
We need to work smart.

We need to work together.
Understand?

**J.P.** *(with WILL above)* Nous avons cent mille hommes ici.
Et nous avons besoin de tout le monde. Nous avons:

Cinquante mille chevaux à nourrir.
Vingt-cinq milles de chemin à construire.
Vingt milles de voie ferrée à déposer.
Vingt-et-un milles de câble à enfouir.
Quarante-cinq milles de tuyaux pour transporter
deux millions de litres d'eau.
Nous devons travailler vite.
Nous devons travailler intelligemment.
Nous devons travailler ensemble.
Comprenez?

**ALL** Oui. Monsieur!

**WILL** They understand?

**J.P.** Oui. Sir.

*Snare.*

*Focus on MIKE.*

**SID** You. Indian.

**MIKE** Yes, sir?

**SID** Back home. You do any, ya know, trapping?

*MIKE just looks at him.*

Care to brush up your skills?

**MIKE** And I run. Every night into enemy lines. Every night
for a month. Listen in, find positions, locate sniper
nests. Crater to crater. Carry the information back.
To artillery, communication trenches, front line. Back
and forth, like I was hunting with Bert.

*Snare.*

**ALL** One, two, three.

**WILL** *(frustrated)* Ahhh.

*Snare.*

*Perhaps they take out their gear.*

| | |
|---|---|
| **MIKE** | *(to CLARE)* Two weeks to Zero Day. |
| **J.P.** | We know what to do. |
| **MIKE** | Gone over it and over it. |
| **SID** | So many times. |
| **MIKE** | Jesus. |
| **SID** | So many times. |
| **J.P.** | Boring. |
| **WILL** | Boring. |
| **MIKE** | Black Line. |
| **J.P.** | Red Line. |
| **WILL** | Blue Line. |
| **SID** | Brown. |
| **J.P.** | We know it! |
| **WILL** | We know it already! |
| **MIKE** | We know it! |
| **SID** | Do it again! |
| **BOYS** | Ahhhh!!!!! |

*The Glide, the digging:*

| | |
|---|---|
| **WILL** | One, two, three, glide… damn! |
| **SID** | Hey, Capt'n. I figure I got this tunnel dug so deep, we should be hittin' Bora Bora by tomorra! |
| **J.P.** | Keep talking, and you'll be diggin' latrines for the rest of the war. |
| **SID** | What about a few graves while I'm at it? |
| **J.P.** | DIG! |

*Snare.*

*They hunker down.*

| | |
|---|---|
| MIKE | *(to CLARE)* One week to Zero. |
| WILL | The week of suffering. |
| SID | Not for us— |
| MIKE | For Fritz. |
| SID | We blast `em— |
| MIKE | Day and night— |
| J.P. | Night and day— |
| WILL | One million rounds. |
| SID | A million rounds. Never seen before. Not even at the Somme. Biggest fireworks display in the world. |
| MIKE | Those cannons, they're the hungry ones. |
| SID | Destroy as much as we can before Zero Day. |
| MIKE | Fritz gets shelled— |
| WILL | Fritz's supplies get cut off. |
| SID | Fritz's got no supplies— |
| WILL | Fritz can't eat; Fritz gets hungry— |
| J.P. | Fritz gets weak. |
| MIKE | Fritz's gonna die. |

*Snare.*

*The Glide, the digging:*

| | |
|---|---|
| SID | Hey! |
| WILL | One, two, three, glide… |

*WILL checks his watch. SID checks the tunnel.*

| | |
|---|---|
| SID | I'M DONE! |
| WILL | I GOT IT! |
| SID | I'M DONE! |
| WILL | I GOT IT, I GOT IT!! |

*The others applaud.*

*Snare.*

MIKE            *(to CLAIRE)* Three days to Zero.

SID             April 6.

J.P.            Good Friday. Communion, boys.

SID             No time.

WILL            No time.

MIKE            Not me.

J.P.            *(with MIKE below)* Notre Père qui es aux cieux... [*Our Father, who art in Heaven...*]

MIKE            Ayo a' pis-to-too-ki, iss-pom-mo-kin-naan nah-kay-ii-ka'-ki-maa-sin-naan. [*Creator, help us to try hard.*]

SID             Whatya doin'.

MIKE            Take the needle, pull it through the skin on your knee, rip off a piece of flesh.

SID             What the—??

*MIKE holds the skin to the sun.*

MIKE            *(with J.P. below)* Ooh-to-kin-naan, A'pis-to-too-ki. [*Hear us, Creator.*] Kaa-mo-taa-ni. [*Grant us safety.*]

J.P.            ...mais délivre-nous du mal. Amen. [*...but deliver us from evil. Amen.*]

MIKE            Some pray to God. Me, I pray to the sun. Pray the fight won't take more than the skin off my knee.

*Snare.*

*Polishing their stuff:*

WILL            Word's in.

MIKE            What.

WILL            Tomorrow. Zero Day.

*Pause.*

| | |
|---|---|
| **MIKE** | So that's it. |
| **SID** | Tomorrow morning. |
| **WILL** | April 9. |
| **J.P.** | Easter Monday. |
| **MIKE** | Well boys... |
| **J.P.** | Well... |
| **SID** | Well. |
| **WILL** | Well... |

*They stare: at their hands, at the ground, anything but each other.*

*Then:*

Time to get ready.

*Snare.*

*Perhaps the Aboriginal drum, increasing its tempo.*

*They load the gear on themselves.*

Ninety pounds of gear:

| | |
|---|---|
| **J.P.** | Check. |
| **SID** | Five sandbags. |
| **J.P.** | Check. |
| **WILL** | Rifle and bayonet. |
| **J.P.** | Check. |
| **MIKE** | Two Mills bombs, 120 rounds. |
| **J.P.** | Check. |
| **SID** | Forty-eight hours rations, filled water bottle. |
| **J.P.** | Check. |
| **WILL** | Ground flare. |
| **J.P.** | Check. |
| **MIKE** | Waterproof sheet, gas mask, goggles. |

| | |
|---|---|
| **J.P.** | Check. |
| **SID** | Pick and a shovel. |
| **J.P.** | Ah come on! |
| **SID** | Pick and a shovel. |
| **J.P.** | Why do we have to—! |
| **SID** | Pick and a shovel! |
| **J.P.** | Okay, okay, check! *Tabouerre…!* |

*Snare.*

*Goods are delivered:*

| | |
|---|---|
| **MIKE** | Two hours to Zero. |
| **WILL** | Boy oh boy, look at this. LOOK at this. |
| **SID** | Jesus. |
| **MIKE** | Holy. |
| **J.P.** | Chocolate. |
| **MIKE** | Cigarettes. |
| **SID** | Chewing gum. |
| **J.P.** | Where'd you—? |
| **WILL** | They sent it down. They sent it down. For us. For us! |

*Snare.*

| | |
|---|---|
| **SID** | One hour to Zero. |
| **J.P.** | Let's go, boys. |

*They go outside.*

*Loud shelling.*

*They need to shout:*

| | |
|---|---|
| **MIKE** | Look at that, would ya. |
| **WILL** | What's that? |
| **MIKE** | The old abbey near Mont St.-Eloi. The steeple, it's ripped in two, like an upside down tooth. |

| | |
|---|---|
| **WILL** | That like "a vision" or something? |
| **MIKE** | Maybe. |
| **J.P.** | I don't care. I'm going over the top and I'm not looking for a blighty. If I'm with the boys in heaven after the battle, I'll be happy. |
| **WILL** | Not me. A nice little bit of shrap right here, and I'll pat myself on the back. |
| **J.P.** | Look: the moon! |
| **SID** | Clouded over now. |
| **WILL** | Starting to rain. |
| **MIKE** | Let's hope it stays that way. |
| **WILL** | The darker the better. |

*The shelling—stops.*

*Silence.*

| | |
|---|---|
| **MIKE** | You hear that? |
| **SID** | It's nothing. It's… |
| **WILL** | It's the larks. |
| **J.P.** | Big deal. |
| **WILL** | But we can HEAR them, we can…. The shelling. It's stopped. |
| **MIKE** | Gotta rest the guns. Like horses. |
| **WILL** | War's gone to sleep. |
| **SID** | Holding its breath. |
| **J.P.** | Fritz? He's gonna be very, very confused. |

*Snare.*

| | |
|---|---|
| **MIKE** | Half an hour to Zero. |
| **SID** | Down the tunnels. |
| **MIKE** | Me, Bentata subway. |
| **J.P.** | Me, Lichfield. |

| | |
|---|---|
| **WILL** | Me, Grange subway. |
| **SID** | Me, Cobourg. |
| **MIKE** | Cold. |
| **WILL** | So cold. |
| **SID** | Subway floor covered with ice. |
| **J.P.** | Smells like piss. |
| **WILL** | No, stale tobacco. |
| **MIKE** | No, sweat. |
| **WILL** | Shh. |
| **MIKE** | Sit down. |
| **SID** | Light a candle. |
| **J.P.** | Quiet now. |
| **MIKE** | Shadows dancing on the chalk walls. |

*Pause.*

| | |
|---|---|
| **WILL** | What'cha doin'? |
| **J.P.** | Carvin' my name. |
| **WILL** | Why? |
| **J.P.** | Wanna leave something behind, don'cha? |

*SID coughs.*

| | |
|---|---|
| **MIKE** | You okay? |

*SID coughs, but nods "yes."*

Writin' a letter?

| | |
|---|---|
| **SID** | Yeah. |
| **MIKE** | Your honey? |
| **SID** | A pal. |
| **MIKE** | Good on ya. What is it? |
| **SID** | *(shows it)* Postcard. |
| **J.P.** | Fifteen minutes. |

| | |
|---|---|
| **MIKE** | Rum rations! |
| **WILL** | Oh yes. |
| **MIKE** | Tot of rum. |
| **WILL** | Oh yes. |
| **SID** | Down the hatch, boys. |
| **WILL** | Courage in a cup. |
| **MIKE** | Fire in your bellies. |
| **J.P.** | À votre bonne santé! [*To your good health!*] |

> *They drink.*
>
> *Then:*

| | |
|---|---|
| **WILL** | Smoke? |
| **MIKE** | Smoke? |
| **SID** | Yeah. |
| **J.P.** | Thanks. |
| **SID** | Need a match? |
| **WILL** | Yeah. |
| **J.P.** | Can you, can you, my hands, they… |
| **WILL** | Thanks. |
| **J.P.** | Thanks. |

> *They light cigarettes.*
>
> *They smoke.*
>
> *Silence.*
>
> *Then:*
>
> *They start to sing.*
>
> *To themselves.*
>
> *Softly, slowly.*

| | |
|---|---|
| **SID** | "When Tommy went across the field to bear the battle's brunt |

|       | Of course he sang this little song, marching to the front |
|-------|-----------------------------------------------------------|
| **WILL** | And when he's walking through Berlin he'll sing the anthem stillHe'll sit down and say, `How are you Uncle Bill' |
| **ALL** | Here we are, here we are, here we are again... |
| **J.P.** | There's Pat and Mac and Tommy and Jack and Joe |
| **MIKE** | When there's trouble brewing— |
| **SID** | When there's something doing— |
| **WILL** | Are we downhearted...? |
| **ALL** | No!<br>Let them all come!<br>Here we are, here we are, here we are again...<br>We're fit an' well and feeling as right as rain<br>Nevermind the weather, now we're altogether<br>`Allo. `Allo. Here we are again..." |

*The song drifts off—into their minds.*

*The men—butt their smokes.*

*They now think, feel, breathe, as one.*

|       |                  |
|-------|------------------|
| **MIKE** | Five minutes. |
| **J.P.** | Pack it up, boys. |
| **WILL** | Let's go. |

*They go into the trenches.*

|       |                  |
|-------|------------------|
| **SID** | Outside. |
| **WILL** | Into the trenches. |
| **SID** | Silence. |
| **J.P.** | Nothin'. |
| **MIKE** | No talking. |
| **J.P.** | Can hear Fritz, he's so close. |
| **MIKE** | Wind's pickin' up. |

| | |
|---|---|
| **WILL** | Starting to snow. |
| **J.P.** | Rats! |
| **SID** | *(itching)* Lice, rats, don't know which I hate— |
| **WILL** | Shhh. |

*Silence.*

*They are breathing heavy now.*

| | |
|---|---|
| **MIKE** | *(whisper)* Two minutes. |
| **SID** | *(whisper)* Fix bayonets. |

*They do so.*

| | |
|---|---|
| **J.P.** | One minute. |

*They wait.*

*And wait.*

*Holding their memories tight.*

*Then:*

*A whistle—pierces the morning air.*

*They all take a sharp breath.*

*LAURIE—appears in the flash of a flare.*

*Darkness.*

**End of Act One**

## ACT TWO

*They wait.*

*A whistle—pierces the morning air.*

*The men all take a sharp breath.*

† † †

*The whistle is LAURIE, fingers in his mouth.*

| | |
|---|---|
| **LAURIE** | G'day. I'm after a gal from Shubenacadie, Nova Scotia. |
| **CLARE** | Oh my God. |

*CLARE—runs to him, hugs him.*

What are you doing here?

| | |
|---|---|
| **LAURIE** | Well, I was on my way to the Western Front see, and I— |
| **CLARE** | You! |
| **LAURIE** | On leave. Let's go. |
| **CLARE** | I can't, I'm on duty all this— |
| **LAURIE** | Taken care of. Matron's given you time off, God bless her, for, what was it, "exemplary duty." Pack your things. |
| **CLARE** | Where are we going? |
| **LAURIE** | The ocean a'course. |
| **CLARE** | The ocean, but that's miles away! |
| **LAURIE** | Borrowed a horse. |
| **CLARE** | Borrowed? |
| **LAURIE** | They'll never know it's gone. And bring a towel. |
| **CLARE** | Towel? |
| **LAURIE** | When's the last time you had a bath, missy. |
| **CLARE** | You're one to talk! |

LAURIE     Nice dip in the sea, some rum...

CLARE     Rum? You borrow that too?

LAURIE     I have every intention of returning it. Along with the horse.

> *A whistle—pierces the morning air.*
>
> *CLARE takes in a sharp breath.*
>
> † † †
>
> *MIKE/CLAUDE has shovel in hand.*

J.P.     Claude, comment ça va? Qu'est-ce que tu fais? [*Claude, how are you? What are you doing?*]

CLAUDE/MIKE     Ça l'air de quoi? [*What's it look like?*] "Shovelling shit."

J.P.     Qu'est-ce qui est arrivé? [*What happened?*]

CLAUDE     J'ai dit: "Sergent, quand pensez-vous que nous irons au front?" [*"Sergeant," I say, "When do you think we'll be called to the Front?"*]

Il dit: "You speak to me in English, Private." Moi je réponds: "Je pensais que c'était un bataillon français." [*I thought this was a French–speaking battalion.*]

J.P.     Ah no...

CLAUDE     Et lui, il dit: "This is a Canadian battalion, Private. We are fighting for the King of England, and you will speak to me in the King's English."

J.P.     *(under his breath)* Trou de cul... [*Asshole...*]

CLAUDE     That's exactly what I said. Asshole.

J.P.     Claude...

> *The next scene may be played in any combination of French or English.*

CLAUDE     "Clean out the latrine," he says. "Clean out the shit. Good practice for the rest of your life."

J.P.     You gotta play by the rules, Claude. You gotta—

**CLAUDE**     NO! I'm not gonna play by their rules! [*NON! Je ne jouerai pas selon leurs règles!*]

       *He throws down the shovel.*

       Why am I here Jean-Paul? I never even wanted to join in the first place! [*Pourquoi est-ce que je suis ici, Jean-Paul? Je ne voulais même pas m'enrôler dans l'armée!*]

       *Pause.*

**J.P.**     ...Claude.

**CLAUDE**     Eh? Is this what you wanted? To see your best friend shovelling Anglo crap `cause he bothered to speak the language of his pa and granpapa?! Eh? [*C'est ça que tu voulais, eh? Voir ton meilleur ami torcher le cul crotté des anglais parce qu'il a parlé la langue de son père et de son grand-père?!*]

       *J.P. is silent.*

       Which language you gonna speak to the Hun, Jean-Paul? Eh? You gonna yell in English or French when you stick your bayonet through him? And when he dies in front of your eyes, that Hun, what then Jean-Paul? You gonna pray in English, my friend? [*Dans quelle langue vas tu parler au Boche? Vas-tu crier en anglais ou en français quand tu vas le poignarder avec ta baïonnette? Et quand il va mourir devant toi, le Boche, quoi donc? Tu vas prier en anglais, mon ami?*]

       *J.P. is silent.*

       Well I'll tell you what, Jean-Paul. If they tell me to go over the top? And I gotta kill a Hun? Know what I'm gonna do? I'm gonna say no. I'm gonna get down on my knees and pray. I'm gonna pray to the God of my pa and your pa and our grandfather and their father before them. I'm gonna pray for forgiveness, Jean-Paul. Et je vais te dire une chose, je vais prier en français. [*And I'll tell you one thing, I'm gonna pray in French.*]

       *A whistle—pierces the morning air.*

*J.P. takes a sharp breath.*

† † †

*The whistle of a chickadee.*

*WILL and SID — on the shores of a lake.*

*They are sweaty and hot.*

**WILL**     Need a rest?

*They stand. Stare at the lake.*

See that?

**SID**     What.

**WILL**     The water here's dark.

**SID**     Yeah.

**WILL**     It's the quartz and granite make it that way.
And over there?
The far shore...?
See that?
Where the lake's cutting into the shore?
Like it's... carving its memory deep into the land.

*SID smiles.*

This lake.
It's got stories.
Somewhere, lurking just beneath the shallows, it's
got stories, but no one to tell them to, no one to write
them down.
Know what I mean?

*SID looks at him.*

**SID**     Know what I like about this place?

**WILL**     What's that.

**SID**     It's warm.

*WILL laughs.*

It's by the water, and it's warm, and all I'm missing
is...

WILL    What?

SID     All I'm missing is a coconut tree.

    *They laugh.*

    *SID lies down.*

    *WILL does the same.*

    *Then:*

    *Flies.*

Stupid flies!

    *SID—waves them away.*

    *Shoos one from WILL's face.*

    *WILL pushes SID away, and they both laugh.*

    *WILL lies back.*

    *Closes his eyes, enjoys the sun.*

    *SID looks at him.*

    *Then:*

    *He reaches out a hand, slowly, gently, `til:*

    *It touches WILL's cheek.*

    *WILL—his eyes remain closed.*

    *He breathes in the moment.*

    *Then:*

    *He looks at SID.*

    *He gets up, slowly.*

    *Picks up his knapsack.*

What... what are you doing?

WILL    Better be getting back.

SID     What do you mean?

WILL    Before it gets dark.

SID     Why? I thought we were...

> *WILL packs.*

Will...

> *WILL packs.*

WILL!

> *WILL stops.*

Did I do somethin'? Did I...?

> *WILL slings the pack over his shoulder.*
>
> *He looks at SID.*
>
> *He can't say it.*
>
> *He leaves.*

...Will?

> *A whistle—pierces the morning air.*
>
> *SID takes a sharp breath.*

† † †

> *A train whistle.*

| | |
|---|---|
| **MIKE** | What happened? |
| **BERT** | Long story. |
| **MIKE** | Got time. |
| | *Pause.* |
| **BERT** | Gassed, brother. |
| **MIKE** | Jesus... |
| **BERT** | No masks. Just piss on a cloth, hold it to your mouth. |
| **MIKE** | That when they send you home? |
| **BERT** | No. Back into the line. |
| **MIKE** | Jesus. And then? |
| **BERT** | Gassed again. |
| **MIKE** | That when they send you home? |

| | |
|---|---|
| **BERT** | Nope. Back into the line. |
| **MIKE** | Jesus, Bert. And then? |
| **BERT** | Gassed again. That's when they sent me home. |

*The train whistle.*

| | |
|---|---|
| **MIKE** | Waited. At the station. Whole reserve. Waitin' for the first Indian veteran to come back. The first warrior. We made a deal: when you came back, I'd go. |
| **BERT** | Caught tuberculosis in the trench. Gassed three times, but it's the T.B. that got me. Gassed three times, but I die on the way home. Go figure. |
| **MIKE** | A week goes by. Another train. This time you're on it. |
| **BERT** | Yeah? |
| **MIKE** | Pry off the coffin lid. |

There you are. Your skin. T.B. and the gas turns it.... All that gangrene, aching to get out.

You wait, Bert. I'm gonna make you proud, brother. I'm gonna be a warrior.

*A whistle—pierces the morning air.*

*MIKE takes a sharp breath.*

† † †

*LAURIE, whistling softly.*

*He and CLARE sit, stare at the ocean.*

| | |
|---|---|
| **LAURIE** | What you thinkin' about? |
| **CLARE** | The cliffs at Fundy. Surrounded by pines. Imagining old Glooscap standing on that spot, making the tide turn 'round in the bay. You...? |
| **LAURIE** | Tryin' to remember what pine trees smell like. |

*She cuddles in his arms.*

| | |
|---|---|
| **CLARE** | Can't I borrow you for a while, like the horse and the rum? |

LAURIE     Could disguise myself as a nurse. Think anybody'd notice?

CLARE     You, a Bluebird?

LAURIE     No? Well then it's the Front for me.

         *He opens the rum, pours.*

CLARE     Where to?

LAURIE     Vimy Ridge.

CLARE     Where's that.

LAURIE     Somewhere in France, I believe.

CLARE     Oh!

         *She slugs him.*

LAURIE     I understand it stands about a hundred and forty-five metres above—

CLARE     Nooooo!

LAURIE     Ahhhh, its the *story* of Vimy you want!

CLARE     You!

LAURIE     Not sure. But when I find out, you'll be the first to know.

         *He pours shots.*

CLARE     Laurie McLean, will you marry me.

         *Pause.*

LAURIE     Where then.

CLARE     Five Islands, overlooking the bay.

LAURIE     Hm. I always had my heart set on Springside Presbyterian in Upper Stewiacke.

CLARE     *(scoffs)* Over my dead body!

LAURIE     Ha!
            Well.
            Sooner mine I'm sure.

> *He drinks.*
>
> *She regards him.*

CLARE    You all right?

LAURIE   Fine.

> *He pours again.*
>
> *She notices this.*

CLARE    How is it.

LAURIE   How's what.

CLARE    How is it. Where you are.

> *LAURIE — hesitates.*
>
> *Then:*

LAURIE   Well, Clare, it's like this...
         We get up `round noon, see.

CLARE    Noon.

LAURIE   Yes, up at noon. Play some cards. Write a letter or
         two to you and Mother.

CLARE    Myself and Mother.

LAURIE   Have a hot, hot shower.

CLARE    Oh yes.

LAURIE   Brunch of steak and eggs.

CLARE    Steak?

LAURIE   And eggs. And after the jigs and reels, it's time for
         Lieutenant McLean to help with a trench raid. No
         matter I'm not in a fightin' unit, no matter, come on
         McLean, we need your help to kill a few Huns! Come
         on then, time to murder some Bosch!

> *She stares at him.*

First thing, Clare, you head into no-man's-land, see?
Crawlin' on your hands and knees through the mud.
Then, ya smoke out some Huns with your Mill's

bombs. And when they come up with their hands up?
Ya mow 'em down with your machine gun, or pick
'em off with your leftover Ross rifle, if you can figure
out how the Jesus-thing works.

*His bitterness and anger grow:*

Next, ya drag a friend out of a crater. Oh, but the
poor bugger's drowned in the muck see, so you best
leave him there to rot. Then ya head back to the line,
but not before pickin' up some pieces of leg or an arm
or a bit of brain. And before you know it, it's time for
tea.

| | |
|---|---|
| **CLARE** | Laurie… |
| **LAURIE** | After that, ya dig a grave or two and… |
| **CLARE** | Laurie, please— |
| **LAURIE** | Oh but it's fun, Clare— |
| **CLARE** | Enough. |
| **LAURIE** | It's so much fun I can't— |
| **CLARE** | Stop! |
| **LAURIE** | WELL?! |

*Pause.*

You wanted a story, didn't ya?

*Pause.*

I ain't the boy you knew when we was kids. And I
ain't the lad you met in Montreal. No. I'm a "man"
now, see. I'm a "man."

So you think long and hard about it, Clare. Because
if you're really after wanting to marry me, then you
better know this. You're not just getting me. You're
getting all the… mess what's inside me now. And it
ain't never going to leave, Clare. Never.

It's stuck.
In here. *(his heart)*
For good.

*LAURIE vanishes.*

*CLARE watches the boys as:*

† † †

*They wait.*

*Hold their memories in.*

*A whistle—pierces the morning air.*

*A loud clap—as if shells bursting.*

*Flares—as if the northern lights.*

*They give a battle yell—all in their own way.*

| | |
|---|---|
| **SID** | 5:30 a.m. |
| **MIKE** | Ten thousand thunders. |
| **J.P.** | Tongues of fire. |
| **WILL** | Lightning ripping up the clouds. |
| **SID** | A rainstorm of metal, sweeping up the ridge. |
| **WILL** | The Creeping Barrage. |
| **J.P.** | The Glide. |
| **WILL** | Keep pace. |
| **SID** | Make sure we don't get too far ahead or too far behind the curtain of fire. |
| **WILL** | One, two, three, glide… |

† † †

*Focus on MIKE.*

*Perhaps the others become shadows in the memory.*

**MIKE**     First scout, I lead my boys through the maze of mud and craters. Make my way to Black Line. First set of German trenches. Throw a Mill's bomb and…

All the Huns come out, their hands up!

*He laughs.*

And I keep going, jumping from shell hole to shell hole, heading to the next target: Red Line.

But then. I get caught. Holes filled with mud, bodies, rats, and I...

I can't get out, I'm stuck, stuck, and I tell the others: keep going, keep going! And I think: "I'm gonna die, I'm gonna drown in all this... death."

Don't move, don't be like an animal stuck in a snare, trying to bite its own leg off, stay calm. Take the bayonet off the gun, use it like a hook, dig it into body after body, drag myself out, like I was climbing a mountain in winter.

I get outta there, catch up. Pass Red Line, heading to Blue Line when I hear it.

That "pop."

Gas.

Can't breathe. And the guy next to me, his face starting to go blue, and I take his respirator, put it on him, and he starts breathing...

Then I put mine on, start breathing, but I, I... gotta pull it off to puke, and put it on again, and pull it off to puke, and put it on again...

Can feel my skin boilin', my lungs burnin', gotta get under it, under the gas cloud, so I lies down, breathe, breathe, breathe.

Lying on Vimy Ridge staring straight up and...

The sky. Red. From the shrap exploding in the air. White from the flares. Green from the gas. Just like, just like...

Oh, Bert...
I failed you, brother.
Nothin' brave about this.

> *MIKE —his injuries returned.*

> *CLARE goes to him.*

† † †

*Focus on J.P.*

*Perhaps WILL and SID become shadows in his memory.*

**J.P.**     Over in Division 2? *(smiles)* We get the show of our lives. The Barrage! Le barrage! Better than any fireworks in Montreal, I tell you.

But when we go over the top... guys move too fast, get caught, go down, screaming...

The stretchers swarming over the field, like ants, ya know? One guy's crying, "water, water," then I see the top of his head, gone. Looks like... the fish roe I used to scoop out at the shop...

But by 11:30, we're at Blue Line. Before I know it, there I am, on top of Vimy Ridge! *(laughs)* Staring at it for so long, hard to imagine what was on the other side. Like when I was a kid, living in the east end, and you never seen the west end, you finally get there, and you think: "wow, this is it, eh?"

*(thrilled)* Two days, and then a week's leave. Two days and I get a break!

    *Pause.*

But next morning, before dawn...

Captain wakes us up. It's dark, but I can see the rays climbing up over the Ridge. To the north, I can make out guys fighting on the Pimple.

Captain marches a few of us off. Five or so guys, don't know any of 'em. 'Bout fifteen minutes later we pass the crosses. I think, grave digging. *(curses, in French)* Sacrament...

But we go right past the graves. Walk into a small field with one small tree. Captain hands us each a rifle. Not suppose to use our own. "Don't look in the cartridge. One of you has a blank."

And then we know.

*Pause.*

They bring the guy down the road, the padre next
to him, two guards holding him on each side. They
bring him in front of us, he lifts his head, and then I, I
see...

*Pause.*

Private Claude Lalancette has been tried for cowardice and for missing battle, and has been declared
guilty, and under military law, is sentenced to death,
by being shot. Do you have any last words?

...Et puis il commence à prier. En français. [...*And he
just starts praying. In French.*]

They blindfold him, tie him to a tree. Captain pins a
white circle to his heart.

And I look at him. And I...

*Hammers being cocked.*

And I...

*Aim being taken.*

They always give one guy a blank, eh.
So you walk away.
Hoping you're not the one. Not the one who—

*Shots—more memory than sound.*

*His hands shake—his illness once again present.*

My hands, they smell like blood, they smell like...

*He weeps.*

...Ah, Claude... pardonne-moi. [*Oh, Claude, forgive
me.*]

*CLARE goes to him.*

† † †

*Focus on WILL.*

*Perhaps SID becomes a shadow in his memory.*

**WILL**  We had two objectives. That's it. Black and Red Lines.
Do that and we get to Hill 145, the very top of Vimy.
A cinch.

I start out. One, two, three glide.
One, two, three, glide.
Like I'm, I'm paddling a great river.

Get to Black Line. And when we do...

*(laughs)* The Huns are running like hell, back over the
other side of the ridge! Never saw it coming!

Except one guy. He, he...

He jumps out at me, eh. And we're standing there,
him and me. Staring at each other, lookin' each other
right in the eye. And I'm thinkin', is he gonna surren-
der? Is he gonna kill me?

So I wait:
One.
Two.
Three...

*Pause.*

And I stab 'im.
My bayonet.
Straight through his heart.
And he looks at me.
His eyes...

*Pause.*

And bang. Right then, something hits me.

Knocks me into a shell hole. My arm, flopped over
like a dead fish. My chest, red as a...

And next to me...

The guy, the German.
Lyin' there.
Dead.
His eyes still open.

Staring at me.
Staring at me.
Ripping at my insides, my...

*Pause.*

And I'm alone.
I'm all alone.
And I don't wanna be alone...

*His injuries return.*

*CLARE goes to him*

† † †

*Focus on SID.*

**SID**  (*positive*) It ain't far to the Pimple. Hundred yards or so. And as we pour over the top, we're yellin' "Go Winnipeg!"

But steep, the Pimple.

Not ten yards, ten yards, and we're pinned. German machine gunners, staring straight down, like it's a shooting gallery.

But whaddya gonna do, eh? So, we keep pressing. Up the field. But it's soggy as spring grass, ya know? Guys, their gear, like an anchor, ya know? Just dragged them down into the shell holes and they...

Ever hear a horse scream?
Nothin' like it.
Except men.
In shell holes.
Drownin'.

*Pause.*

But we push our way up, and then we realize. Jesus. We're under fire not only from the FRONT, but from the FLANK, and the REAR.

Christ. We're pinned. Ain't goin' nowhere. Dig all the tunnels I want, not diggin' myself outta this one. No sir.

Stay there all morning. All afternoon. 'Til early evening. 'Til the sleet stops. 'Til the sun starts setting.

And then.
We see 'em.
Comin' up on our flank.
On our right.

Highlanders.

*LAURIE is there.*

*CLARE draws in a breath.*

Everybody knows 'em. The Highlanders Without Kilts. Never a real fightin' unit, never even belonged to a brigade. Ditch diggers and work horses. Biggest bunch of ugly ducklings ya ever seen.

And here they come. Run up Vimy like they know every crater. Charge up like they've been climbing mountains all their lives. Scramble over the sea of mud like it was smooth sailing. And they took it, boys. In an hour. In an hour, those Highlanders took the Ridge.

And I seen them.
Waving at us.
Wavin' from the top of Vimy.
Wavin' like they were kids on a snowbank.

*He falls.*

Somethin' hits. Wake up, I'm in a crater, and...

I can't see, I can't see!

I got guys on top of me, and I, I can't get any air.

...Get 'em off me, get 'em off me!!

*His injuries begin to return.*

(driven) And somebody pulls me out. Drags me out from underneath. Pulls me onto his lap.

**LAURIE**  Buddy...

**SID**  He says.

| | |
|---|---|
| **LAURIE** | Buddy… |
| **SID** | Yeah? |
| **LAURIE** | Where ya from? |
| **SID** | Winnipeg. I'm from Winnipeg. |
| **LAURIE** | You're gonna be okay. |
| **SID** | Yeah? |
| **LAURIE** | We done it, eh? Us Highlanders. |
| **SID** | Yeah, you guys done it all right. |
| **LAURIE** | I was at the top. |
| **SID** | Yeah? |
| **LAURIE** | I was at the very top. *(to CLARE)* It's in my memory now. It's all stuck in here. |
| **SID** | And I could feel him, so warm, like, like I was… |

And then.

> *A shot.*
>
> *LAURIE vanishes.*

Nothing.

Feel over to his face. Blood. And he goes cold. So cold…

> *CLARE—holds her hand to her mouth.*

But I was so warm…. Will?

| | |
|---|---|
| **WILL** | Yeah? |
| **SID** | I was warm. |

> *They all help SID to his bed.*
>
> *CLARE—slowly leaves.*
>
> *Silence.*
>
> *They don't know what to do, what to feel.*
>
> *Then:*

*SID starts to sing.*

*They all join, slowly, quietly.*

SID       *(barely audible)* "The poets since the war began have written lots of things.... About our gallant soldier lads which no one ever sings.

J.P.       Although their words are very good, the lilt they seem to miss.

MIKE       For some we like the tricky song, the song that goes like this:

ALL       Here we are, here we are, here we are again...

J.P.       There's Pat and Mac and Tommy and Jack and Joe

MIKE       When there's trouble brewing

J.P.       When there's something doing

WILL       Are we downhearted...?

ALL       No!
Let them all come.

*The boys sing with growing tempo and intensity, except SID.*

Here we are, here we are, here we are again...
We're fit an' well and feeling as right as rain.
Nevermind the weather, now we're altogether
`Allo. `Allo. Here we are again..."

*They laugh, cry—with relief.*

J.P.       Boy oh boy!

WILL       What I wouldn't give for a Labatt's now, eh?

MIKE       Or a Lowney's!

WILL       Or a bowl a' Saskatoons!

J.P.       Or some salt beef!

*They laugh.*

MIKE       Eh, Sid?

*SID does not respond.*

**MIKE** ...Sid?

**WILL** ...Sid?

*WILL goes to him.*

*SID is dead.*

*MIKE—turns on his side.*

*J.P.—goes somewhere, staring.*

*WILL—props up SID's head in his lap.*

...Sid?

Aw, Sid...

*WILL—gently touches SID's cheek.*

✝ ✝ ✝

*Time passes.*

*SID slowly vanishes.*

*Then:*

✝ ✝ ✝

*Day.*

*CLARE—enters with mail.*

*She obviously hasn't slept.*

**CLARE** *(tired)* Mornin'.

**MEN** *(distracted)* Mornin'.

**CLARE** *(stoic)* Mail call.

**J.P.** Mail?

**CLARE** Saunders?

*WILL does not respond.*

*She places it on his bed.*

Metivier.

| | |
|---|---|
| **J.P.** | Thanks. |
| **CLARE** | Goodstriker. |
| **MIKE** | Nice for a change. |
| **CLARE** | And... |
| | *(curious)* ...Me. |
| | *She sits, considers opening the letter.* |
| **MIKE** | Oh no, no... |
| **WILL** | What is it? |
| | *MIKE hands the letter to WILL. He reads.* |
| **J.P.** | What's it say? |
| **WILL** | Distinguished Conduct Medal. |
| **J.P.** | ...Mike... |
| **WILL** | "...Private Goodstriker risked his own life to aid another soldier with his gas mask..." |
| | *MIKE shakes his head.* |
| **J.P.** | C'est pour le courage, Mike. [*It's for bravery, Mike.*] And you... you paid the price, eh? |
| | *Pause.* |
| **MIKE** | *(to J.P.)* You? |
| **J.P.** | *(not happy)* Discharge. |
| **MIKE** | J.P., you're goin' home. |
| **J.P.** | Je ne sais pas comment je vais faire... [*I don't know how I'm gonna...*] |
| | *J.P. looks away.* |
| **MIKE** | *(to WILL)* You? |
| | *WILL has finally looked at it.* |
| | *He stares at MIKE—speechless.* |
| | What is it? |

*WILL holds it up.*

**WILL**  …Postcard…

*The men sit in sadness.*

*CLARE opens her letter.*

† † †

*LAURIE appears—young and healthy again.*

*He speaks to her.*

**LAURIE**  April 9, 1917. Somewhere in France.

Dear beady-eyed beauty! Well, I guess we Highl'nders are just too good to be sittin' back staring at Vimy. Seems like there's a job to do, that only us Nova Scotia boys can handle. Isn't it always the way! So we're going over the top this afternoon.

And when I come back, I'm gonna have some story to tell, Clare. We're gonna get married on the cliffs at Five Islands, and we're gonna sit there, watching old Glooscap turn the tide backward, and I'm gonna tell you the story of Vimy. I'm gonna tell you the story of Vimy over and over and over. 'Til we're old and grey.

*From away—thunder.*

*CLARE—speaks to LAURIE.*

**CLARE**  Oh, Laurie…

Take me back.

Take me back to Five Islands.

Take me back to the bay.

I'll sit on the cliffs, and I'll smell the pines, and I'll watch the sea rush in, and I'll imagine.

Us. There. Together.

Laurie…?

Let's go home.

*LAURIE smiles.*

*He and the other men slowly vanish:*

*The thunder—draws closer.*

*But it is clear now:*

*It is the thundering of guns.*

**End of Play**

✝

# Afterword

Historians have argued that the Battle of Vimy Ridge symbolizes the birth of Canada as a nation. It certainly marks a defining memory for Canadian identity and patriotism. More than ninety-seven thousand Canadians prepared doggedly for the battle of Vimy Ridge and on Easter weekend 1917, fifteen thousand went over the top. While all are remembered as victors, 3,598 perished and 10,602 survived as casualties. The statistics are numbing and serve as reminders of the cost of dedication, loyalty, courage, triumph and sacrifice. These noble qualities and conditions often render war a romantic yet tragic abstraction. Wars are fought by folks made up of flesh and blood. They are people with fathers and mothers, lovers and wives and husbands, brothers and sisters, and children. War infects us all—with tears, relief, anticipation and dread. We all hope for victory but most importantly we all hope our friends and loved ones will return safely.

Vern Thiessen's *Vimy* is not an historical play that falls victim to authenticity and distracting detail. Rather, the play is a poetic fiction set against a momentous historic moment—the Battle of Vimy Ridge—a uniquely Canadian victory in the Great War.

Thiessen's play is about six individuals—their attempts to remember and most importantly to heal. His characters elicit empathy and compassion—characters that resonate truthfully. They take us on an emotional journey shedding light on our present by way of our past. Among them: a dutiful nurse who finds strength through her romantic memories; a young Maritime soldier who reminds us all about sacrifice; a naive French Canadian recruit torn between patriotism and cultural loyalties; an Aboriginal volunteer whose warrior heritage ennobles a white man's war; a sensitive prairie infantryman whose unique sense of comradeship is awakened; and a solitary and withdrawn boy-soldier from the Ottawa Valley. All these characters are driven to remember—to remember their battles within and the battle for Vimy itself.

New plays are always a risk but a risk worth taking over and over again. We all believe the process of development will minimize those risks. But really, the process of getting the play from the page to the stage is often alchemical. There is no scientific equation offering definitive results. Experiential and philosophical speculations run rampant; but the one thing we know for sure is that the playwright fields every opinion, suggestion, caution, negation and admiration thrown at him or her. Making sure the story is effectively and dramatically told is the ultimate goal. In this case the process has been rigorous and thorough. Thiessen has nurtured this story along for nearly four years—he's had moments of doubt and concern, and moments of inspiration and confirmation. Along the way he has rarely veered away from the vital and memorable characters he's created. His task has been to find and refine the cadence of the play, the language of his characters, the truthfulness of their interactions, and his dramatic elegy to a defining moment in Canadian history.

—Brian Dooley

Vern Thiessen is one of Canada's most-produced playwrights. His plays have been seen across Canada, the United States, Asia, the United Kingdom, the Middle East and Europe. Well-known works include *Vimy*, *Shakespeare's Will* and *Apple*. *Einstein's Gift*, *A More Perfect Union* and *Lenin's Embalmers* have all been seen off-Broadway. His plays for young audiences include *Bird Brain*, *Dawn Quixote* and *Windmill*. With composer/collaborator Olaf Pyttlik he has created two musicals, *Rich* and *Rapa Nui*. Thiessen is also the author of several adaptations, including *Wuthering Heights*. He is the winner of many awards including the Governor General's Literary Award, Canada's highest honour for playwriting. Thiessen is a past president of the Playwrights Guild of Canada and of the Writers Guild of Alberta. He splits his time between Canada and New York City.